Dances With Tears

Also by Efrayim Levenson

For My Relations
Buffalo, NY: Poetrymanz Press, 2000

Jewish America: A Brief History of a One-Sided Love Affair
Kindle Editions, 2010

Funhouse
Hoboken, NJ: Poets Wear Prada, 2013

Dances With Tears

Efrayim Levenson

POETS WEAR PRADA • Hoboken, New Jersey

Dances With Tears

Copyright © 2007, 2013 Efrayim Levenson

All rights reserved. Except for use in any review or for educational purposes, the reproduction or utilization of this work in whole or in part in any form by electronic, mechanical or other means, now known or hereafter invented, including xerography, photocopying and recording, or in any informational or retrieval system, is forbidden without the written permission of the publisher:

    Poets Wear Prada
    533 Bloomfield Street, Second Floor
    Hoboken, New Jersey 07030
    http://pwpbooks.blogspot.com

First North American Publication 2007
First Mass Market Paperback Edition 2013

The poem "& Ribbon" originally appeared in *For My Relations* (Buffalo, NY: Poetrymanz Press, 2000).

ISBN-13: 978-0-9817678-3-3
ISBN-10: 0-9817678-3-4

Printed in the U.S.A.

Front Cover Image: Roxanne Hoffman
Author Photo: Marissa Levenson

Dedicated to:

R. Shmaryahu Charitonow
for showing me my foundation

R. Eli Blokh and R. Yossi Mendelson
for teaching me how to build on it

my daughter Marissa
for loving me in spite of myself

Table of Contents

& Ribbon	*3*
Morontyme	*4*
Dance of the Barking Rabbit	*5*
Mountain Dance	*6*
Electrocuted Tears	*7*
Mordechai's Day at the Beach	*8*
Temple	*9*
Rain Dance	*10*
Tomorrow Will Sparkle	*11*
From This Day Forward	*12*
Glossary	*13*
About the Author	*15*

Dances With Tears

& RIBBON

& I died a little every time you cried & screamed at our nose-to-nose screams & I moved to the city where the noise is quiet & Mommy would not let me go until she took you home, her home & we invented a new life & we won & you lost & we lost & we are a 5-minute phone call every Monday night & you're in my arms, my home, 18 hours a month & you remember less and less of your hometown & you lose baby teeth without me & you grow taller without me & you do not learn to ride your bicycle without me & though I have love I am a lonely old man without you & I am not a Daddy without you & all I have are snapshots without you

MORONTYME

In a moment of blondness
I can lose my mind
faster than the speed of sound
to those nether places
where mysterious death hides
at the root of happy vegetation

Duh duh duh

One snap of the synapse
brings me back
and another takes me away

I forget over the miles
in moments of unforgivable blondness

I'm out of sight
out of my mind
a sacrificial semiconscious lamb
years in the making

Can my town breathe today?
Only the haze knows

Give me a cigarette quick
so I can see the breath
I can't believe

Watch your toes
while I dance
the Morontyme jig

My swinging legs and arms
lose their minds
in fits of joyful idiocy
in moments of uncontrollable blondness
that shimmer like a summer river
at sunset

DANCE OF THE BARKING RABBIT

I dance on the broken wind
that erases the spirit in my body
the hope in my mind

It's the waltz
I wouldn't wish
on the last escapee of a saddened ghost town
not far from here

I smell the grayness burn holes
through the light
coming in the night

I dare to breathe its name
as it hops and scurries
from tree to tree to
work in the traps of Death's love

"This is more fun
than any hooray can cry"
is its whispered reply

My bed is a giant skateboard
that flies down the highway
listening to car music
as it survives every crash and pothole

"Get out of the way!
I'm going nowhere fast!"
the destiny of my birth
I'm so happy

I wish I could steer
back to the dance floor
of dissonant compulsion
under a short-circuited mirror-ball
but the wet whirlwind skipped town
right under my blur

The dance alone burns between my legs

MOUNTAIN DANCE

As the sun rises over the tree line
children of G-d are thankful for another chance
to breathe the wealth of His *chesed*
till the field of His *tzedek*
sow the produce of His *emes*

May I have this dance?

The music of our lives
is the rhythm of our souls
the best we can hope for on short notice

Love is the blood
that courses through our veins of faith
the song that soothes nightmares

Dance with me
It's my last chance to show
what 2 right feet can do

How do you love so much
the incessant dichotomy that shares your bed?

How hard must worlds collide
before the chaff falls away?

How soft must kisses be
before they pierce stone?

May I have this hoedown dance?
Maybe the band will play
a swingin' shuffle next

Just don't bop your head off
before you lay it down to rest to pray to dream
of a peaceful home
a hideaway from the frenzy

The dance steps are lighter more agile and free
on the mountain where silence breathes a smile

Come dance on the mountaintop with me

ELECTROCUTED TEARS

The world in here
HaShem out there
One and the same
is miles apart
Changes don't reconcile
every day
Alone with you alone
the space between togetherness

And yet I try to live
without a cloud encompassing
If only this window faced the black west
sometimes blue
If I cried
my tears would sound like yours
A guitar with no strings
remembers how to sing

Love endures
a mouth faster than eyes
a mind quicker than pen
a smiling portrait of decay

Incomplete Efrayim
is my name in rare places
I am *kelipat nogah*
brighter than *rasha*
much less than *benoni*

If we wash our hands
and breathe our *kepittel*
our love becomes an answered prayer
If we don't
we give birth
to an empty questioned soul

MORDECHAI'S DAY AT THE BEACH

The brightness of Your surf
sings in the place in my soul
where the past rides
the wave to the future

Automatic men in my memory
smile at the beauty
of this hidden beach of stone

It's been a long time
since I've been home
among the noisemakers
drowning out the name
of our malicious enemy
of long ago

I can feel the first
niggun of my rebirth
welling up in my chest
closed eyes rocking around
the *farbrengen* table

Wine and stronger
push us to our dancing feet
and swinging arms
to enlighten our celebration
of knowing no difference
between good and evil
a confirmation of our confusion
only the knowledge of *HaShem*
can assuage

TEMPLE

I rise above the smoke and ash
in the easy rhythm
of your love's embrace

The stars' twinkle in your eyes
releases me
from the noise in the void

Lay with me on the forest's floor
We'll sing *tehillim* to *Shamayim*
Niggunim to the *Or Ein Sof*
and laugh with the birds' replies

The sun shines in our hearts
through the heavy threat
of snow white clouds

You touch me
in the air we breathe
I hear your soul call
from miles apart

Come home to me
Come home

RAIN DANCE

I will dance under a rain-filled sky
and dream of sun-soaked sand
that buries my footprints
as I walk home to peace
in a quiet heart that sings
of everything 6 strings can give
to a life in need of the nurture
of a pipe enemies can smoke as friends
on a free bridge to the depths of joy
where we swim together in love
with the music of a perfect day

TOMORROW WILL SPARKLE

Tomorrow will sparkle
in preparation for *Shabbos*
a prelude to harmony
a song at the edge of bliss

Here comes the Queen
her crown of radiance
protected by a snood

FROM THIS DAY FORWARD

Before the movement of sky
before the height of trees
before the songs of birds and frogs
before the heat and light of fire
before my growing faith in *HaShem*
I pledge my life and love to you

Glossary
(in order of appearance)

chesed: kindness

tzedek: righteousness

emes: truth

HaShem: "The Name", i.e., G-d

kelipat nogah: "the shell that shines", i.e., the good that's within evil

rasha: wicked, wickedness

benoni: "intermediate", i.e., that place between righteousness and wickedness

kepittel: psalm

niggun: a Chasidic wordless song (pl. – *niggunim*)

farbrengen: an informal gathering of Chasidim for the purpose of telling Chasidic stories and singing *niggunim*

tehillim: psalms

Shamayim: Heaven

Or Ein Sof: "Light of Infinite Oneness", i.e., G-d

Shabbos: Sabbath

About the Author

Efrayim (Fred Barry) Levenson began writing poetry in Buffalo, New York, in 1982. He has been published in small press anthologies across New York State, as well as in Missouri and Belgium, and has collaborated with musicians Dave Schmeidler, Rey Scott, and others.

Levenson's poetry writing path has been guided by Joy Walsh, Allen Deloach, Robin Kay Willoughby, and Carole Southwood. His work is influenced by poets Lawrence Ferlinghetti and Allen Ginsberg, musicians Frank Zappa and Buckethead, and by Chabad Chasidism.

Levenson's imagery ranges from the subtlety of a quiet walk in the park to an attack by a runaway lawnmower. His poems are montages of rhythm in which he plays with rhymes and the sounds of words. Deloach once said, "See through the eyes with the heart." Efrayim Levenson's poetry will take you on a journey into his heart and soul.

www.ingramcontent.com/pod-product-compliance
Lightning Source LLC
Chambersburg PA
CBHW061520040426
42450CB00008B/1706